PROBES

by Ruth Owen

PowerKiDS press™

New York

Published in 2015 by **The Rosen Publishing Group, Inc.**
29 East 21st Street, New York, NY 10010

Library of Congress Cataloging-in-Publication Data
Owen, Ruth.
Probes / by Ruth Owen.
p. cm. — (Objects in space)
Includes index.
ISBN 978-1-4777-5846-5 (pbk.)
ISBN 978-1-4777-5845-8 (6-pack)
ISBN 978-1-4777-5847-2 (library binding)
1.Space probes — Juvenile literature. 2. Outer space — Exploration —
Juvenile literature. I. Owen, Ruth, 1967-. II. Title.
TL795.3 O94 2015
629.43—d23

Produced for Rosen by Ruby Tuesday Books Ltd
Editor for Ruby Tuesday Books Ltd: Mark J. Sachner
US Editor: Sara Antill
Designer: Emma Randall
Consultant: Kevin Yates, Fellow of the Royal Astronomical Society

Photo Credits:
Cover, 1, 5 (center), 5 (bottom), 6–7, 9, 11, 13, 15, 17, 19, 21, 23, 24–25, 27, 29
© NASA; 5 (top), 10–11, © Shutterstock.

Manufactured in the United States of America
CPSIA Compliance Information: Batch # CW15PK: For Further Information contact
Rosen Publishing, New York, New York at 1-800-237-9932

CONTENTS

EXPLORATION AND DISCOVERY

For decades we have been making incredible discoveries about our solar system.

We've learned that a trip to Venus would mean instant death, while Mars could one day become a new human world. We've seen rings of ice and rock, discovered volcanoes, and even found a hidden ocean on a distant moon. None of this would have been possible without space probes.

A probe is a spacecraft that travels beyond Earth's **orbit** to carry out scientific investigations. A probe might visit a moon, a planet, a **dwarf planet**, an **asteroid**, or a comet. It might study interplanetary space, the regions around the Sun, and other objects in our solar system. There is even one probe, *Voyager 1*, that has traveled beyond our solar system and is studying **interstellar space**.

A probe does not carry astronauts. It may be remotely controlled by scientists on Earth. It can also be programmed to work autonomously, carrying out investigations without human help and transmitting data millions or billions of miles (km) back to Earth.

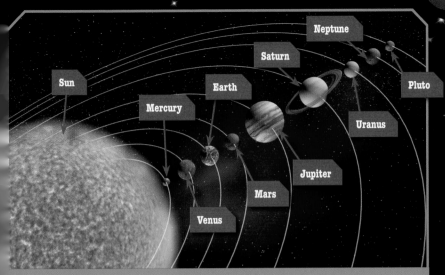

Sun

Mercury

Earth

Venus

Mars

Jupiter

Saturn

Neptune

Uranus

Pluto

Our solar system is made up of the Sun, eight planets, dwarf planets (such as Pluto), moons, and other rocky objects including asteroids. This diagram of the solar system is not to scale.

An illustration of *NEAR Shoemaker.*

NEAR Shoemaker recorded scientific data about Eros. It took photos that showed the asteroid was covered in craters and house-sized rocks.

Crater

A photo of Eros.

SPACE OBJECTS FACT FILE

In 2000, the *Near Earth Asteroid Rendezvous–Shoemaker (NEAR Shoemaker)* probe visited and studied an asteroid named Eros. The probe even landed on Eros and gathered data that showed scientists what **elements** make up the asteroid.

THE *VOYAGER* PROBES

In 1977, two space probes, *Voyager 1* and *Voyager 2*, were launched by NASA on a mission to visit the solar system's outer planets.

The *Voyager* probes are identical and are each about the size of a small car. They are fitted with cameras and a range of scientific instruments.

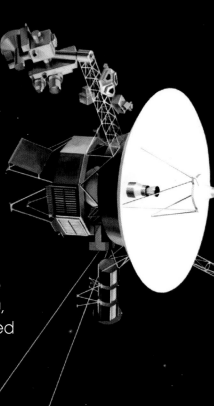

The *Voyagers'* missions were possible because the orbits of the planets Jupiter, Saturn, Uranus, and Neptune were **aligned** in a way that only happens every 175 years. This rare alignment allowed the *Voyagers* to visit a planet and then use the gravity of that planet like a slingshot to propel them on to the next planet.

Voyager 2 launched from the Kennedy Space Center at Cape Canaveral, Florida, on August 20, 1977. *Voyager 1* actually launched after *Voyager 2* on September 5, 1977. *Voyager 2* got its name because, even though it launched first, it would be the second of the two spacecraft to arrive at Jupiter.

SPACE OBJECTS FACT FILE

Many probes have **solar panels** and are powered by the Sun. Scientists knew the *Voyagers* would travel too far from the Sun to use solar power. Each *Voyager* carries a generator powered by **radioactive** plutonium. Heat from the plutonium fuel is turned into electricity to power the probes.

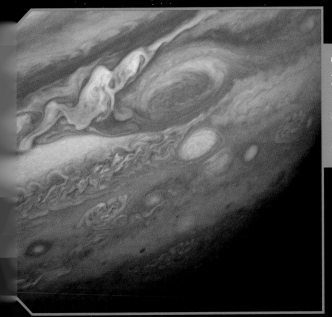

This photo of Jupiter's Great Red Spot was captured by *Voyager 1*. The spot is a giant storm that measures about 15,500 miles (25,000 km) by 7,500 miles (12,000 km).

An illustration of a *Voyager* space probe.

AN INCREDIBLE JOURNEY

In March 1979, *Voyager 1* reached Jupiter. *Voyager 2* reached the planet in July 1979.

Voyager 1 captured images of Jupiter's moons Ganymede, Callisto, Europa, and Io. This allowed astronomers to see the surfaces of these moons for the first time.

In November 1980, *Voyager 1* flew by Saturn. The probe discovered Saturn's moons Prometheus, Pandora, and Atlas. Just under a year later, in August 1981, *Voyager 2* visited Saturn, giving astronomers back on Earth another chance to see Saturn, its moons, and its icy, rocky rings up close.

Originally, the plan was that the two spacecraft would only visit Jupiter and Saturn. They functioned so successfully, however, that their missions were extended.

In January 1986, *Voyager 2* reached Uranus. It discovered 10 new moons and recorded wind speeds on the planet of 450 miles per hour (724 km/h). Finally, in 1989, *Voyager 2* reached Neptune. It discovered previously unknown moons and rings of dust, ice, and rock orbiting the planet. Without *Voyager 2*, very little would be known about Neptune.

SPACE OBJECTS FACT FILE

The Voyager probes travel through space at a speed of approximately 34,000 miles per hour (55,000 km/h).

Voyager 2's flyby of Uranus lasted for just five and a half hours. It took this photo of the planet.

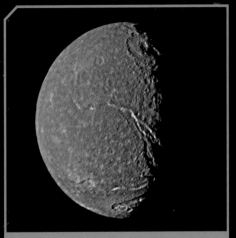

A *Voyager 2* photograph of Titania, Uranus's largest moon.

Voyager 2 flew by Neptune's moon Triton. It discovered the moon has cryovolcanoes, or ice volcanoes. It is one of the coldest places in the solar system.

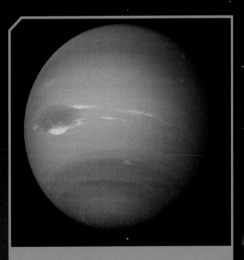

Neptune photographed by *Voyager 2*.

A VOYAGE INTO THE UNKNOWN

The *Voyager* space probes are still going strong! In August 2012, *Voyager 1* left our solar system. *Voyager 2* will soon follow.

Heading in different directions, the two probes will head out into our **galaxy**, the Milky Way. Designed and built in the 1970s, and with onboard computers many thousands of times less powerful than a smartphone, the *Voyagers* have traveled farther than any object that has ever left Earth. What will happen to the little probes?

In case the *Voyagers* ever encounter an alien civilization, each probe carries a gold-plated copper disk containing information about humans and Earth. In about 40,000 years time, *Voyager 1* will fly close to another star. By the way, close in galactic terms means about 9 trillion miles away!

Scientists expect that the two probes will continue to send data back to Earth for another 20 or 30 years. Then their power sources will run out. The *Voyagers* will hopefully continue to fly through space, though. Maybe even forever.

SPACE OBJECTS FACT FILE

The disks aboard *Voyager 1* and *Voyager 2* contain photos of Earth, sounds, greetings in many languages, pieces of music, and scientific information. The equipment to play the disks, which are similar to vinyl records, is also aboard the probes.

The cover of a *Voyager* disk

A *Voyager* disk

It's mind-boggling to think that maybe many thousands, or millions, of years from now, the little *Voyagers* could make contact with intelligent alien life. What will those other beings make of life on Earth in the 1970s?

MARS PROBES

Many spacecraft have been sent to Mars to study the planet. By the end of 2014, four probes were orbiting and studying Mars.

When the orbits of Earth and Mars bring the two planets close together, it can take as little as six months for a spacecraft to reach Mars.

The longest-serving Mars probe is NASA'S *2001 Mars Odyssey*. It reached Mars in October 2001, and was originally scheduled to work for 917 days. *Mars Odyssey* studies the planet's **climate** and geology, or rocks. *Mars Odyssey* has sent information about **radiation** on Mars back to Earth. This data will help scientists make plans to keep astronauts safe if humans ever visit Mars. The probe also transmits messages from **rovers** working on the surface back to Earth.

In June 2003, the European Space Agency (ESA) launched *Mars Express*. The probe reached Mars in December of that year. *Mars Express* searches for water beneath the planet's surface and takes high-resolution images of the planet in color and in 3-D.

SPACE OBJECTS FACT FILE

A tiny sample of carmaker Ferrari's famous red paint traveled on the *Mars Express*. As it traveled away from Earth, the probe reached speeds of more than 6,700 miles per hour (10,800 km/h). That's much faster than any red Ferrari has ever traveled on Earth!

An illustration of *Mars Odyssey* flying over Mars's south pole.

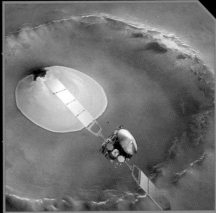

This photo of ice in a 22-mile-wide (35 km wide) crater on Mars was captured by *Mars Express*. An illustration of *Mars Express* has been added to the picture.

This fantastic 3-D view from inside Valles Marineris, a giant canyon on Mars, was created on a computer. In places the canyon is 4 miles (6.4 km) deep. Images from *Mars Odyssey* were used to help build the image.

MORE MARS PROBES

NASA's *Mars Reconnaissance Orbiter (MRO)* began studying Mars in November 2006.

As the probe orbits Mars, it looks for evidence that there were once seas on the planet. Today, there are no rivers, lakes, or oceans on Mars, but MRO and rovers on the surface have found evidence that liquid water once flowed on the planet. Today, Mars's climate is dry and very cold. Scientists believe, however, that Mars was once wet and warm. The *MRO* studies Mars's climate to look for clues that the planet has undergone a dramatic climate change.

The *MRO* also has a powerful camera on board. It can take sharp images of objects on the surface that are just the size of a beach ball. The probe uses this camera to identify interesting places for rovers to study and safe places where they can land.

In September 2014, NASA'S *MAVEN* probe began orbiting Mars. *MAVEN* will study Mars's atmosphere to help scientists understand the climate change that took place on the planet.

SPACE OBJECTS FACT FILE

MAVEN stands for the *Mars Atmosphere and Volatile EvolutioN* mission. The probe will orbit close to Mars's surface. It will study Mars's atmosphere just 93 miles (150 km) above the planet's surface.

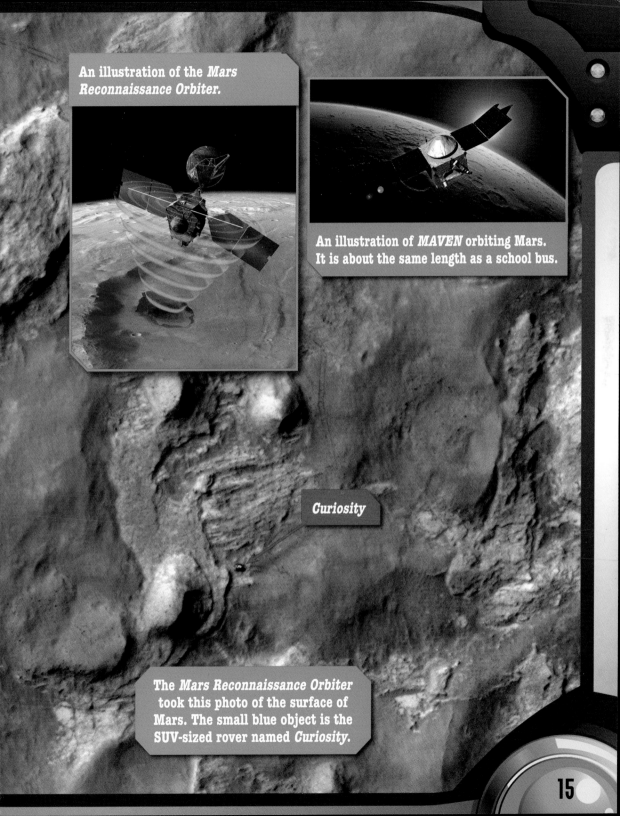

An illustration of the *Mars Reconnaissance Orbiter*.

An illustration of *MAVEN* orbiting Mars. It is about the same length as a school bus.

Curiosity

The *Mars Reconnaissance Orbiter* took this photo of the surface of Mars. The small blue object is the SUV-sized rover named *Curiosity*.

GALILEO GOES TO JUPITER

In October 1989, the NASA probe *Galileo* was launched on a mission to orbit and study Jupiter. The probe was named for Galileo, the Italian astronomer who discovered Jupiter's largest moons.

While it was still close to Earth, the *Galileo* probe made a very important discovery. From out in space, it was able to detect signs that there is life on Earth!

Galileo found clues in the sunlight passing through Earth's atmosphere that showed plants were using light for photosynthesis. It detected large amounts of oxygen, because plants are constantly making this gas. And it detected radio waves that contained human-made information, which showed an intelligent life-form had created them. Being able to detect these signs of life is important for the future. One day, probes or other scientific devices could look for the same clues on distant planets far beyond our solar system.

In July 1995, when *Galileo* was still about 50 million miles (80 million km) from Jupiter, it released a smaller probe that plunged into Jupiter's **atmosphere**. The probe studied the temperature, pressure, and chemical composition of the giant planet's atmosphere.

SPACE OBJECTS FACT FILE

The smaller probe released by *Galileo* transmitted data back to *Galileo* for 58 minutes before it was crushed, melted, or vaporized by the extreme conditions in the gas giant's atmosphere.

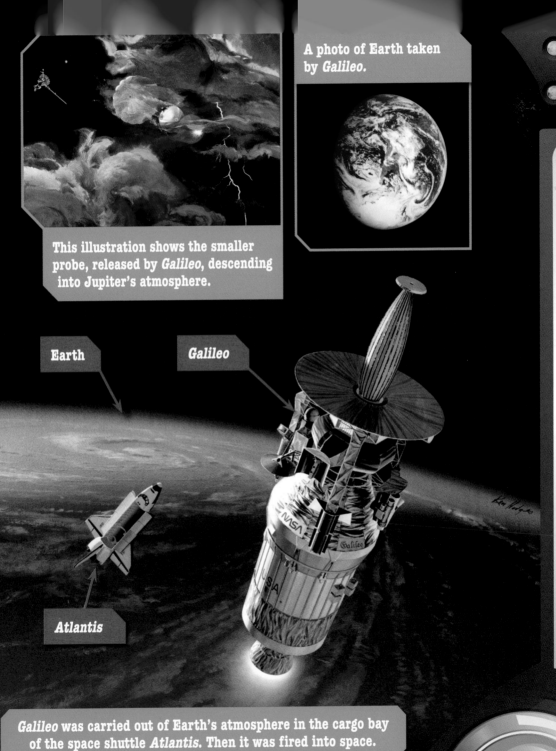

This illustration shows the smaller probe, released by *Galileo*, descending into Jupiter's atmosphere.

A photo of Earth taken by *Galileo*.

Earth

Galileo

Atlantis

Galileo was carried out of Earth's atmosphere in the cargo bay of the space shuttle *Atlantis*. Then it was fired into space.

GALILEO'S DISCOVERIES

In December 1995, *Galileo* finally entered Jupiter's orbit and began its study of the planet and its moons.

Galileo discovered that Jupiter is made of similar amounts of the gas helium as the Sun. When it studied Jupiter's moon, Europa, *Galileo* found evidence that there might be a deep ocean of salt water beneath the moon's icy surface.

In 2003, *Galileo*'s mission was coming to an end. Its fuel supplies were running low. It did not have enough fuel to escape the gravity of Jupiter and its moons and head off into space. Scientists were worried that *Galileo* might eventually crash, perhaps into Europa. They could not risk this happening because if Europa has liquid water, it could mean that there is some form of life on the moon. If *Galileo* crashed into Europa, however, it could contaminate, change, or damage the moon's environment.

So *Galileo* was sent toward Jupiter. The probe headed into the planet's thick atmosphere and disintegrated. After 14 years in space, *Galileo*'s mission was over.

SPACE OBJECTS FACT FILE

Galileo observed huge thunderstorms on Jupiter. Many had lightning strikes that were 1,000 times more powerful than lightning on Earth!

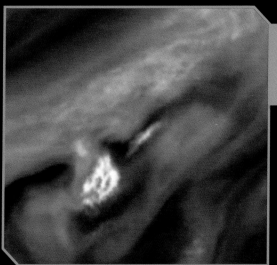

A photo taken by *Galileo* of a vast thunderstorm (the white area) on Jupiter.

This illustration shows *Galileo* flying by Jupiter's moon, Amalthea.

CASSINI-HUYGENS

Saturn is an enormous gas giant planet. It is surrounded by rings of rock, ice, and dust. Some of the pieces of rock are the size of mountains.

In October 1997, NASA launched *Cassini*, the first probe to orbit Saturn. *Cassini*'s mission was to study Saturn and its moons.

After nearly seven years of traveling across the solar system, *Cassini* began orbiting Saturn in July 2004. To reach its orbiting position, *Cassini* had to fly through a gap in Saturn's rings. The probe was named for Jean-Dominique Cassini, an Italian scientist who discovered the widest gap in Saturn's rings.

Aboard *Cassini* was a car-sized landing craft called the *Huygens* probe. Named after Christiaan Huygens, the first person to observe Titan, Saturn's largest moon, the probe was destined to land on Titan. Because *Huygens*' engineers did not know what lay beneath Titan's thick atmosphere, *Huygens* was designed to land on a hard surface or on water.

On December 24, 2004, *Cassini* released the *Huygens* probe.

SPACE OBJECTS FACT FILE

More than 5,000 people were involved in the various stages of the *Cassini-Huygens* mission.

Scientists carry out tests on the completed *Cassini-Huygens* probe.

The *Huygens* probe

This DVD contains 616,400 signatures of people around the world. It was carried into space aboard the *Cassini* probe.

REVEALING TITAN'S SECRETS

Scientists were particularly interested in studying Saturn's largest moon, because of its structure and atmosphere.

Titan is similar to how Earth may have been in the time when life on Earth began. Studying Titan could reveal secrets about the history of our own planet. Titan has been difficult to observe because it is hidden behind a thick atmosphere of gases that even today's high-powered telescopes cannot penetrate.

Using parachutes to slow its descent onto Titan's surface, the *Huygens* probe touched down on January 14, 2005. As it descended through Titan's thick atmosphere, *Huygens* transmitted data back to Earth via *Cassini*. After landing, it continued to transmit information and images for nearly one and a half hours. Finally, scientists on Earth could see the previously hidden surface of Titan.

Since 2004, the probe *Cassini* has continued to send a daily stream of information back to Earth about Saturn and its moons. Today, *Cassini* is still in orbit, and its mission will continue until 2017.

SPACE OBJECTS FACT FILE

Data from the *Cassini-Huygens* mission shows that Saturn's moon Titan probably has an outer layer of ice. Beneath the ice is an ocean of liquid water.

This photograph of Saturn and its rings was created from a series of images captured by *Cassini*.

This image of Titan was created from pictures captured by *Cassini*. It shows the moon's thick atmosphere.

This photo of Titan's surface was taken by the *Huygen*'s probe.

NEW HORIZONS

The tiny, dwarf planet Pluto orbits the Sun in a distant region of the solar system called the Kuiper Belt. The Kuiper Belt is a place beyond the orbit of Neptune where there are many icy objects.

New Horizons blasts off from Earth.

On January 19, 2006, the *New Horizons* probe roared into space atop an Atlas V rocket from Cape Canaveral, Florida. *New Horizons* will reach Pluto in 2015. If the mission is successful, it will be the first probe to perform a flyby of Pluto and its five known moons.

New Horizons should fly within 6,200 miles (10,000 km) of Pluto and 17,000 miles (27,000 km) of Pluto's moon Charon. At those close-up distances, the images of our most famous dwarf planet should be extraordinary.

In 2016, *New Horizons* will begin flybys of other space bodies in the Kuiper Belt, including some that may eventually become classified as dwarf planets.

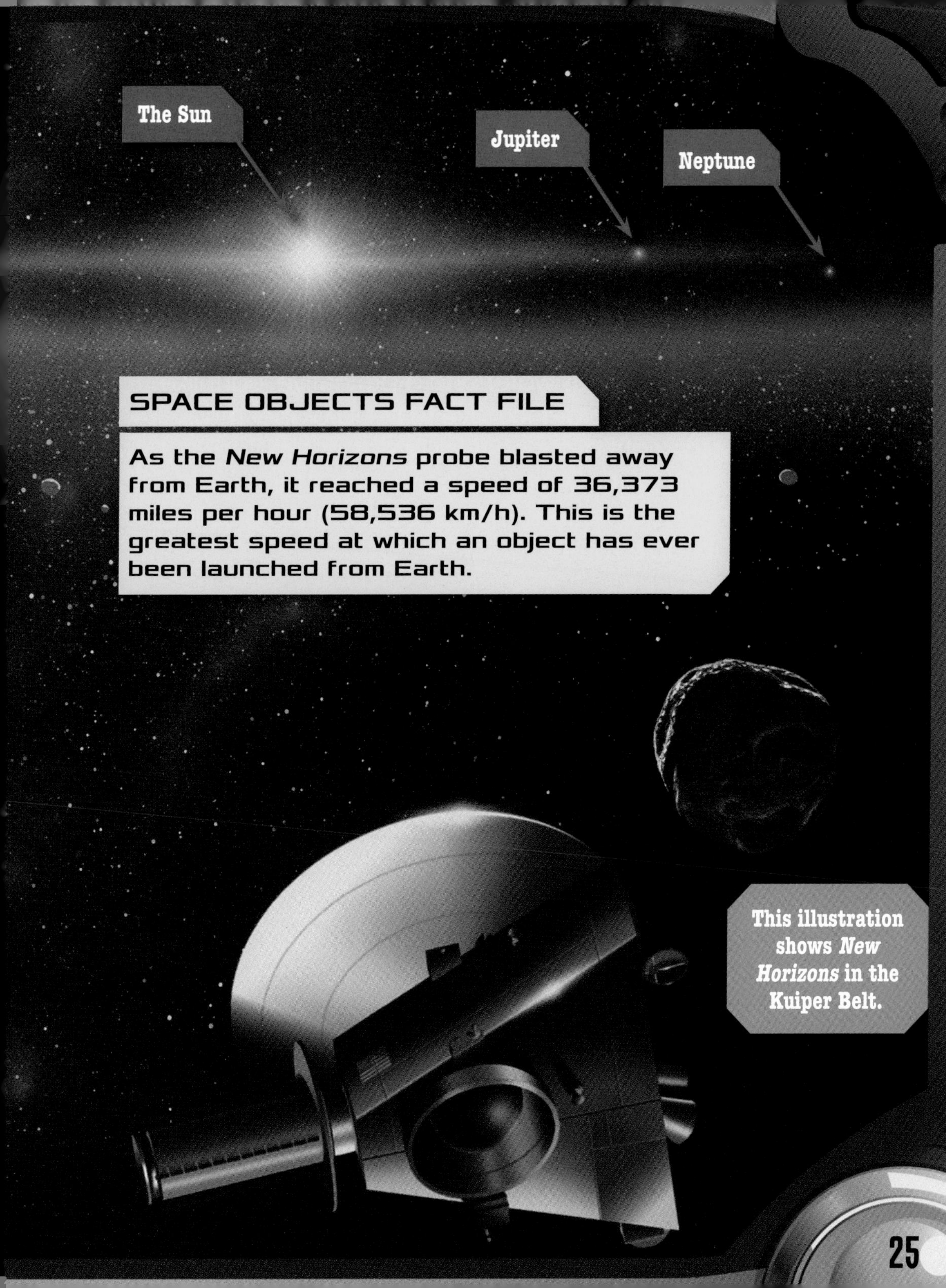

The Sun

Jupiter

Neptune

SPACE OBJECTS FACT FILE

As the *New Horizons* probe blasted away from Earth, it reached a speed of 36,373 miles per hour (58,536 km/h). This is the greatest speed at which an object has ever been launched from Earth.

This illustration shows *New Horizons* in the Kuiper Belt.

SEARCHING FOR EXOPLANETS

Could there be another Earth somewhere in the universe?

In order to be an earthlike planet that could sustain life, a planet needs water and a protective, earthlike atmosphere. In order to have water, a planet must be just the right distance from its star, or sun. Too close, and all the water evaporates. Too far away, and the water freezes. This perfect distance is called the habitable zone.

NASA's Kepler Space Observatory is a probe and telescope designed to look for planets, and in particular earthlike planets, that are orbiting stars beyond our solar system. These distant planets are known as exoplanets. If we look to the sky, however, even the most enormous, brightest stars look like tiny pinpricks of light. So it's a huge task to find a planet that gives off no light and will be many times smaller than its star.

Kepler's mission has been to monitor about 150,000 stars in our Milky Way galaxy. Throughout most of its mission, it has watched for miniscule changes in the star's light as something passed in front of the star. This "something" could be a planet. Many more observations are then needed to confirm if the dimming of the star's light is caused by a passing planet.

This picture shows how Venus (the black dot) looks as it passes in front of the Sun. Kepler watches stars that are many trillions of miles (km) from Earth for this type of event.

An illustration of Kepler in space. The probe follows Earth in an orbit similar to that of our planet around the Sun.

SPACE OBJECTS FACT FILE

The changes in a star's light that Kepler must detect are tiny. Scientists have described it as being like standing several miles (km) from a car and being able to see a flea crawl across the car's headlight!

ANOTHER EARTH?

As of late 2014, Kepler, supported by teams of scientists on Earth, had confirmed the discovery of 989 exoplanets in the Milky Way. Many more are likely to be confirmed, however, in the years to come.

In April 2014, a truly momentous discovery was announced. An Earth-sized exoplanet had been found orbiting in its star's habitable zone. Its position means it could have liquid water on its surface. Named Kepler-186f, the planet is believed to be rocky. That's all we know for now!

Unfortunately, visiting a distant, newly discovered Earth is not within our current capabilities. For example, Kepler-186f is about 3,000 trillion miles (4,800 trillion km) from Earth. It would take hundreds of thousands of years to reach it. New probes and other devices can be used, however, to study the planet from afar.

Kepler has experienced some malfunctions, but its mission has been modified so it can continue planet-hunting and investigating space.

SPACE OBJECTS FACT FILE

Some scientists have estimated that there could be billions of earthlike planets in habitable zones within our Milky Way galaxy. With an estimated 100 billion other galaxies in the universe, it seems very likely that we are not alone!

An illustration of how Kepler-186f might look as it orbits its star.

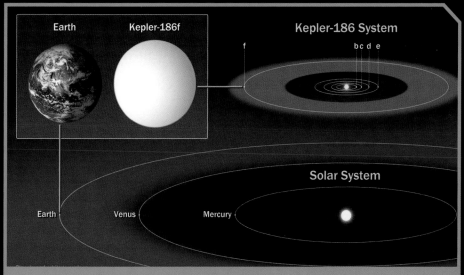

Earth   Kepler-186f

Kepler-186 System

f

bc d e

Solar System

Earth   Venus   Mercury

This diagram shows Kepler-186f's system compared to Earth's solar system. The labels b, c, d, and e indicate other planets.

GLOSSARY

aligned
(uh-LYND) Placed or arranged in a straight line.

asteroid
(AS-teh-royd) A rocky object orbiting a star and ranging in size from a few feet (m) to hundreds of miles (km) in diameter.

atmosphere
(AT-muh-sfeer) The layer of gases surrounding a planet, moon, or star.

climate
(KLY-mut) The average temperature and weather conditions in a particular place over a long period of time.

dwarf planet
(DWAHRF PLA-net) An object in space orbiting the Sun that has a rounded shape but is not a moon of a larger planet. A dwarf planet's orbit will not have been swept clear of other bodies as is the case with the larger, main planets.

elements
(EH-luh-mentz) Chemical substances that consist of only one type of atom and cannot be broken down into simpler substances by a chemical reaction.

galaxy
(GA-lik-see) A group of stars, dust, gas, and other objects held together in outer space by gravity.

interstellar space
(in-tur-STEL-ur SPAYSS) The regions and matter in space between solar systems.

NASA
(NAS-ah) The National Aeronautics and Space Administration, an organization in the United States that studies space and builds spacecraft.

orbit
(OR-bit) The pathway an object takes around another object in space. Also, to move, or circle, around another object in a curved path.

radiation
(ray-dee-AY-shun) Energy that is radiated in waves, such as light from the Sun, or in particles, such as radiation from plutonium.

radioactive
(ray-dee-oh-AK-tiv) Giving off radiation.

rovers
(ROH-vurz) Robotic, wheeled vehicles used to explore a planet or moon.

solar panels
(SOH-ler PA-nulz) Panels made up of a number of solar cells that capture the Sun's energy and use it to make power, such as electricity.

solar system
(SOH-ler SIS-tem) The Sun and everything that orbits around it, including planets (and their moons), asteroids, meteoroids, and comets.

universe
(YOO-nih-vers) All of the matter and energy that exists as a whole, including gravity and all the planets, stars, galaxies, and contents of space.

WEBSITES

Due to the changing nature of Internet links, PowerKids Press has developed an online list of websites related to the subject of this book. This site is updated regularly. Please use this link to access the list: www.powerkidslinks.com/ois/probes

READ MORE

Kops, Deborah. *Exploring Space Robots*. Minneapolis, MN: Lerner Publishing Group, 2012.

O'Hearn, Michael. *Awesome Space Robots*. North Mankato, MN: Capstone Press, 2013.

Snedden, Robert. *How Do Scientists Explore Space?* Chicago: Raintree, 2011.

INDEX

THE PROBLEM WITH EARLY CLOCKS

OOPS!

BY RYAN NAGELHOUT

Gareth Stevens
PUBLISHING

Please visit our website, www.garethstevens.com. For a free color catalog of all our high-quality books, call toll free 1-800-542-2595 or fax 1-877-542-2596.

Library of Congress Cataloging-in-Publication Data

Nagelhout, Ryan.
The problem with early clocks / by Ryan Nagelhout.
p. cm. — (Bloopers of invention)
Includes index.
ISBN 978-1-4824-2768-4 (pbk.)
ISBN 978-1-4824-2769-1 (6 pack)
ISBN 978-1-4824-2770-7 (library binding)
1. Clocks and watches — History — Juvenile literature. I. Nagelhout, Ryan. II. Title.
TS542.5 N34 2016
681.1'13—d23

First Edition

Published in 2016 by
Gareth Stevens Publishing
111 East 14th Street, Suite 349
New York, NY 10003

Designer: Sarah Liddell
Editor: Ryan Nagelhout

Photo credits: Cover, p. 1 Jonathan Kantor/Stone/Getty Images; p. 5 DEA/G. CIGOLINI/Contributor/ De Agostini/Getty Images; p. 7 (Roman calendar) Leemage/Contributor/Universal Images Group/ Getty Images; p. 7 (Mayan calendar) Vadim Petrakov/Shutterstock.com; p. 9 (main) Three Lions/ Stringer/Hulton Archive/Getty Images; p. 9 (sun clock) Dorling Kindersley/Getty Images; p. 11 Dmitri Kessel/Contributor/The LIFE Picture Collection/Getty Images; p. 13 (candle clock) Heliocrono/Wikimedia Commons; pp. 13 (main), 15 (main) Print Collector/Contributor/Hulton Archive/ Getty Images; p. 15 (pendulum clock) Science & Society PIcture Library/Contributor/SSPL/ Getty Images; p. 17 (main) Zbynek Jirousek/Shutterstock.com; p. 17 (inset) Matt Cardy/Stringer/ Getty Images News/Getty Images; p. 19 (diagram) Encyclopaedia Britannica/Contributor/Universal Images Group/Getty Images; p. 19 (quartz watch) turtix/Shutterstock.com; p. 21 SCIENCE SOURCE/ Science Source/Getty Images.

Printed in the United States of America

CPSIA compliance information: Batch #CS15GS: For further information contact Gareth Stevens, New York, New York at 1-800-542-25onathan

CONTENTS

Words in the glossary appear in **bold** type the first time they are used in the text.

TELLING TIME

Do you know what time it is? Maybe you're wearing a watch on your wrist or there's a clock on the wall. Being able to tell time is important. Maybe you have to go to bed at a certain time or need to make sure you don't miss your favorite show on TV.

Most clocks we use today are **mechanical**, but what about a clock that uses the sun or water to tell time? Let's check out all the wacky ways people have told time throughout history.

OOPS!

Metrology is the science of measurement. Clocks are used to measure time. If you measure it wrong, you'll never know what time it really is!

THIS IS AN EXAMPLE OF WHAT THE INSIDE OF A MECHANICAL CLOCK LOOKS LIKE.

USING THE SKY

One early method of telling time was using a calendar, not a clock. Ancient people—such as Sumerians living in Iraq, Syria, and Iran more than 5,000 years ago—used the moon to track time. Their calendar had 30 days in a month, and each day had 12 periods that lasted 2 modern hours.

The Mayans, living in Central America between 2600 BC and AD 1500, made a 260-day and a 365-day calendar using the moon, the sun, and the planet Venus.

OOPs!

One cycle of the Mayan calendar ended on December 21, 2012. Some thought that meant the world was going to end!

6

ancient Roman calendar

THE 12 PERIODS OF A SUMERIAN DAY WERE BROKEN DOWN INTO 30 DIFFERENT PARTS, WHICH EACH EQUALED 4 MINUTES OF OUR TIME.

Mayan calendar

SUN CLOCKS

Ancient Egyptians used the sun to tell time. They built obelisks, which are tall, four-sided towers that get narrower as they rise. As the sun rose and set, the obelisk created a shadow on the ground that moved. Putting marks on the ground around the obelisk that matched the shadows, the Egyptians could tell what time of day it was. This is also called a sundial.

Egyptians also made a sun clock, which was portable, or could be moved. It measured shadows with a raised **crosspiece** at one end.

OOPs!

Sun clocks need shadows to work. If it's nighttime or it's cloudy out, you can't tell what time it is!

EGYPTIANS MADE THE FIRST
SUN CLOCK AROUND 3500 BC.

obelisk

sun clock

WATER WORKS

Water clocks were one way people measured time without using the sun. One of the oldest water clocks made was found buried with an Egyptian king. **Archaeologists** think it was made around 1500 BC.

A common kind of water clock was made from two bowls. One bowl sat above the other, and **gravity** helped the water flow out. Some had markings on the higher bowl that showed how much water had flowed out. Others had marks in the lower bowl to show how much water had flowed in.

OOPS!

It's very hard to control the flow of water, which meant water clocks weren't as **accurate** as other, later clocks.

GREEKS CALLED WATER CLOCKS "CLEPSYDRAS," WHICH IS GREEK FOR "WATER THIEVES."

11

GREAT CANDLES

Alfred the Great is sometimes credited with inventing the candle clock. Alfred was a king in England from AD 871 to AD 899. He kept time with six candles that burned for 4 hours each.

Alfred used the candles to keep track of how much time he spent on eating, sleeping, praying, studying, and kingly duties. Adding a weight, like a nail, to a candle clock meant it could be used as an alarm. When the candle burned through, the weight fell and made a noise!

OOPS!

Early candles had wicks that didn't burn away. They had to be cut off, or the heat from the burned wick could melt the wax and set the alarm off early!

THE CANDLE CLOCK WASN'T ACTUALLY INVENTED BY ALFRED THE GREAT. USING A CANDLE TO TELL TIME WAS MENTIONED IN CHINESE WRITING DATING BACK TO AD 520.

candle clock

13

WEIGHT FOR IT

Christiaan Huygens, a Dutch scientist, made a pendulum clock in 1656. A pendulum is a weight that swings back and forth at the end of a pole. The length of time each swing takes depends on how long the pendulum is. A pendulum's motion moves other weights or springs. They make the hands on a clockface move.

On a clockface, the short hand tracks hours and the long hand tracks minutes. Early weighted clocks became less accurate as their springs got stretched out. They would need to be wound again.

OOPs!

The early weighted clocks that hung on walls were so heavy they fell and broke. Finally, pendulum clocks were put in cases standing on the ground.

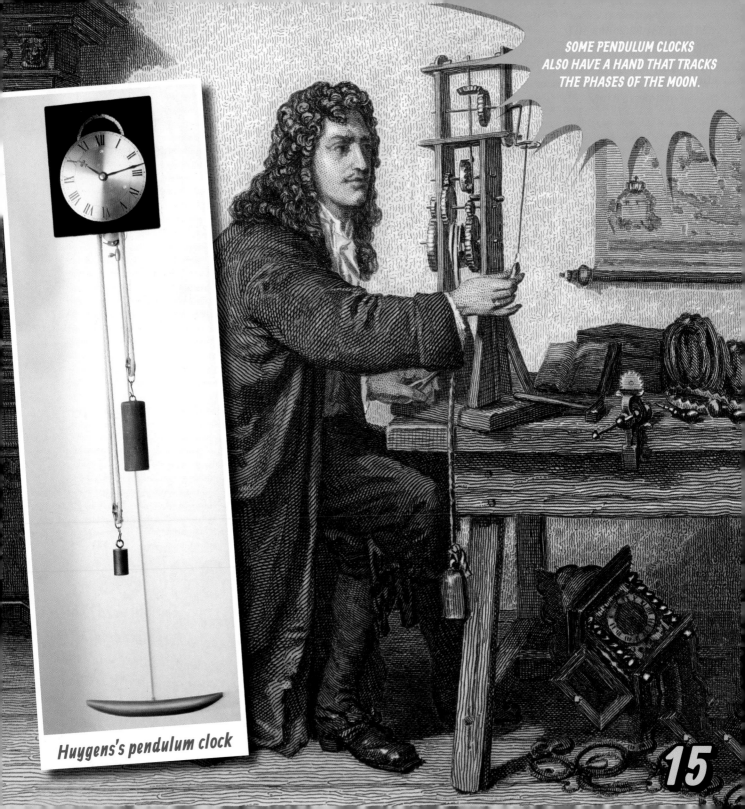

SOME PENDULUM CLOCKS ALSO HAVE A HAND THAT TRACKS THE PHASES OF THE MOON.

Huygens's pendulum clock

15

WHEELS IN ACTION

Mechanical clocks became more accurate with the help of moving gears called a wheelwork. People would wind the clock, which powered the wheelwork and moved the clock's hands.

The large main wheel connects to a smaller one that in turn connects to smaller and smaller gears. One gear rotates, or spins, once per hour to track hours. A smaller gear tracks minutes, rotating once per 60 seconds. Other gears track other things, but all the parts work together smoothly.

OOPs!

Many clocks still need to be wound to keep time accurately. You can often hear a ticking clock and see if it is moving too fast or too slow.

WHEELWORKS WERE USED TO MAKE MANY WATCHES, BUT THEY CONSTANTLY NEEDED WINDING TO KEEP WORKING.

world's oldest mechanical clock

USING CRYSTALS

In the 1920s, clocks started using a crystal called quartz. Quartz is used as an **oscillator**, which keeps the clock moving at a certain rate. This made quartz watches and clocks more accurate.

Electricity is sent through the crystal and used to power the clock itself. Quartz watches are only off about 1 second every 10 years! Most quartz used in watches today is synthetic, or man-made. It's made watches cheaper to make.

OOPS!

Quartz watches often get their energy from a battery. You need a new battery when it runs out of energy or the watch stops working.

QUARTZ IS ONE OF THE MOST COMMONLY FOUND MINERALS ON EARTH. A MINERAL IS MATTER IN THE GROUND THAT FORMS ROCKS.

HOW A QUARTZ WATCH WORKS

hour hand

minute hand

battery

quartz oscillator

motor

circuit board

19

ATOMIC CLOCKS

The best machines used to keep time today are called atomic clocks. Atomic clocks measure the movement of tiny atoms to tell time. Most clocks use an **isotope** named cesium 133. Clocks using cesium 133 measure the number of times a cesium atom moves around in an excited state, or frequency.

Some scientists are working with **lasers** to make something called an **optical** clock. This clock measures 430 trillion light waves per second and is even more accurate than an atomic clock.

OOPs!

In 1967, scientists decided 1 second was the length of time it takes a cesium atom to move 9,192,631,770 times between two specific energy levels.

GLOSSARY

accurate: free from mistakes

archaeologist: a scientist who studies past human life and activities

crosspiece: something placed so as to cross something else

cycle: a period of time marked by certain events

gravity: the force that pulls objects toward Earth's center

isotope: one of two or more forms of atoms in the same element

laser: a narrow beam of light energy

mechanical: having to do with machines

optical: relating to vision

oscillator: a device that creates an electric charge

FOR MORE INFORMATION

BOOKS

Somervill, Barbara A. *The History of the Clock*. Chanhassen, MN: The Child's World, 2005.

Spilsbury, Richard, and Louise Spilbury. *The Clock*. Chicago, IL: Heinemann, 2012.

Woods, Michael, and Mary B. Woods. *Ancient Computing Technology: From Abacuses to Water Clocks*. Minneapolis, MN: Twenty-First Century Books, 2011.

WEBSITES

Building a Water Clock
sciencenetlinks.com/lessons/building-a-water-clock/
Build your own water clock with the help of this great site.

Official US Time
time.gov
Find out the official time in different parts of the United States and where the sun is shining on Earth.

INDEX